HOW TO DRAW
MAGICAL THINGS

for Kids

ALLI KOCH

Paige Tate & Co.

Copyright © 2023 Alli Koch
Published by Paige Tate & Co.
PO Box 8835, Bend, OR 97708
contact@bluestarpress.com
www.bluestarpress.com

Written and illustrated by Alli Koch

ISBN: 9781958803554

Printed in Colombia

10 9 8 7 6 5 4 3 2

this book
BELONGS TO

_____

LET'S DRAW!

The nice thing about being an artist is that you can make the rules. Everyone has their own style, which is why your drawings will look different from someone else's. In this book, each animal is broken down into steps. My goal is to help you see the simple parts of what may seem like a hard thing to draw.

We will start with the most basic outline or guide and work our way up. You will start to see a pattern with each animal we draw; starting with simple guidelines, then breaking down "C" and "S" shape lines, and lastly erasing the unneeded lines for the finished look. Don't forget to draw your lines lightly first so it is easier to erase them. My favorite thing to say when drawing is:

If it was perfect, it would not look handmade!

I cannot wait for you to get started. Happy drawing!

TOOLS

The cool thing about art is that you can use any tool you want! Yep, that's right! You are the artist, so feel free to be creative. For this book, let's keep it simple. It's easy to learn using either blank sheets of paper or grid paper.

When you are learning to draw, you really only need a pencil and a good eraser. To follow the step-by-step instructions: draw everything lightly, then go over your lines with whichever tool you would like to use. You can use different pens, markers, colored pencils, or even crayons to add details to your animals.

CIRCLES CAN BE TRICKY. TRY USING A PENNY OR A CIRCLE STENCIL TO HELP!

BREAK IT DOWN

Anyone can draw! If you can write your ABCs (which I am pretty sure you can do!), then you can draw everything in this book. Each magical thing can be broken down into a bunch of "C" and "S" shaped lines. Almost everything that is round is two simple "C" lines put together. An "S" line is for when something has a dip or curvy line.

All of these magical things are broken down into six steps. What you will draw in each step will be a black line, what you have already done will be in gray lines. There are more than 40 magical things in this book for you to learn how to draw. The chapter dividers in this book are also bonus coloring pages that you can color!

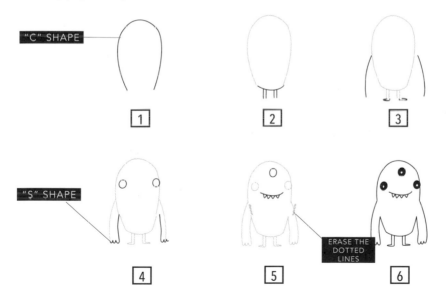

"C" SHAPE

1

2

3

"S" SHAPE

ERASE THE DOTTED LINES

4

5

6

FANTA-SEA

MERMAID

Mermaid tails are like mood rings—they change colors based on the mermaid's mood!

1

2

3

4

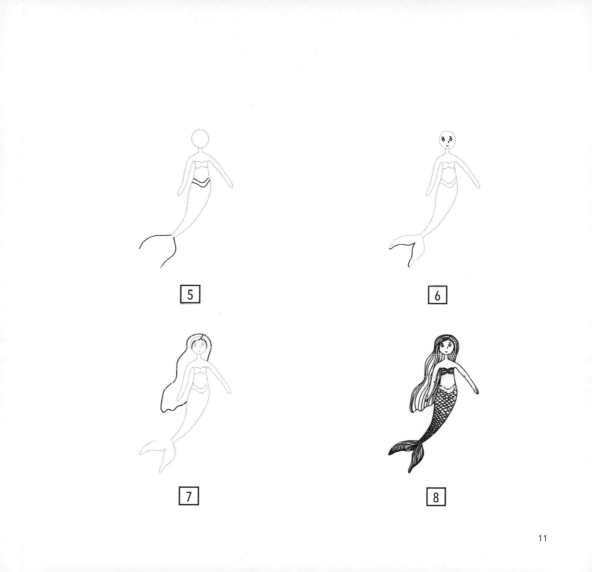

5

6

7

8

MERMAN

Like their female counterparts, legend says that a merman can summon storms and sink sailors' ships.

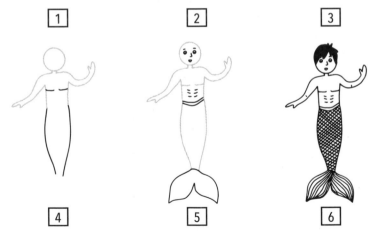

TREASURE CHEST

When finding hidden treasure, maps were more valuable than gold for many pirates.
Maps would allow them to navigate through difficult waterways!

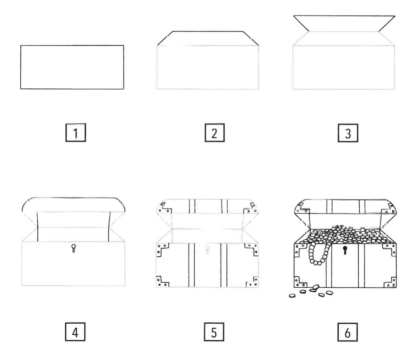

SEA DRAGON

With their sharp teeth and ability to swim fast, sea dragons pose a deadly threat to sailors in popular folklore and mythology.

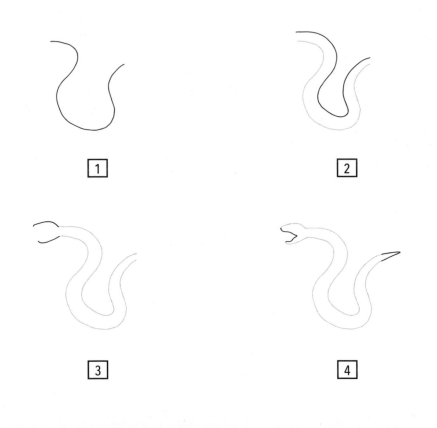

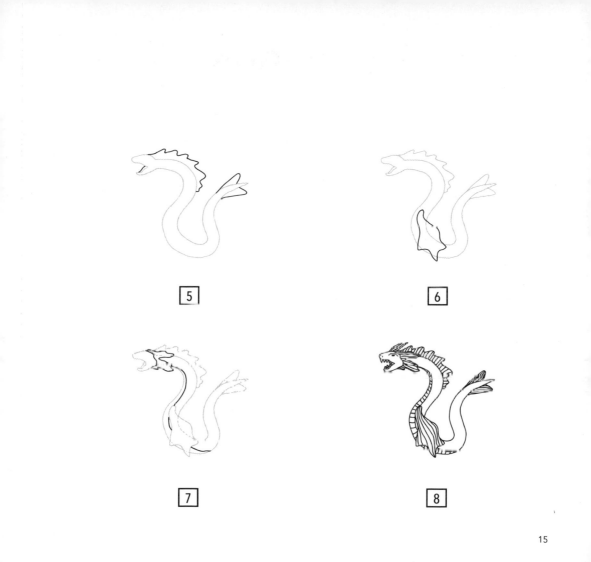

5

6

7

8

SHELL WITH PEARL

Pearls are considered gemstones,
making them the only gemstones to come from a living creature.

TRIDENT

In Greek mythology, Poseidon could use his trusty trident to create thunderstorms.

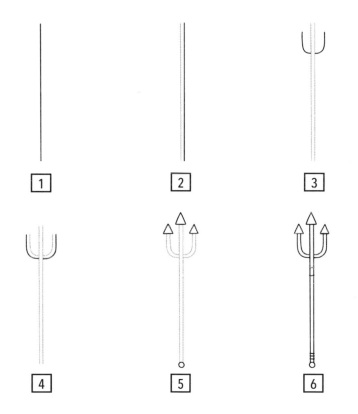

FAIRY TALE

CASTLE

There are more than 10,000 castles or castle ruins in Europe alone.
The oldest castle that people still live in was built 1,000 years ago!

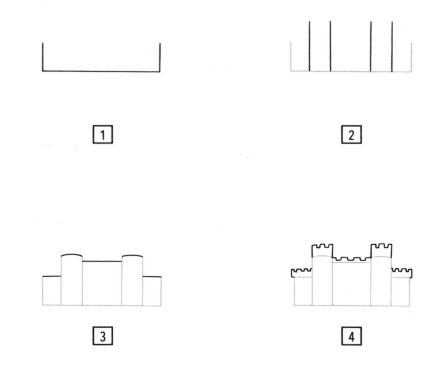

1

2

3

4

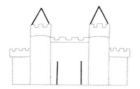

5

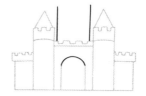

6

7

8

KNIGHT

Knights used to wear full-body armor. Since the armor was usually made of metal, it was very heavy and difficult to move in.

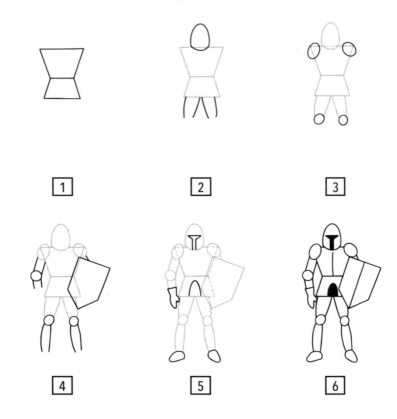

PRINCESS

Did you know there was a real-life princess who was also an Oscar winner?
Grace Kelly won an Academy Award before she became Princess of Monaco.

PRINCE

Historically, the eldest prince was the automatic heir to the throne.

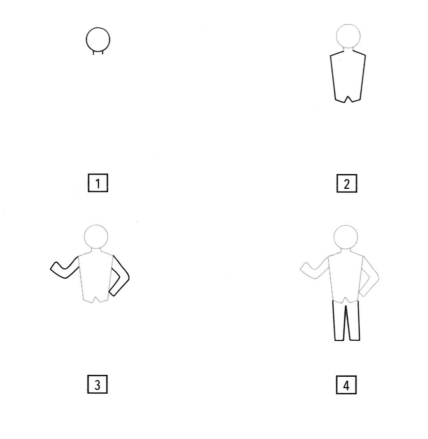

5

6

7

8

SLIPPER

In some versions of the fairy tale, Cinderella's slippers were
made of gold, silver, or even fur!

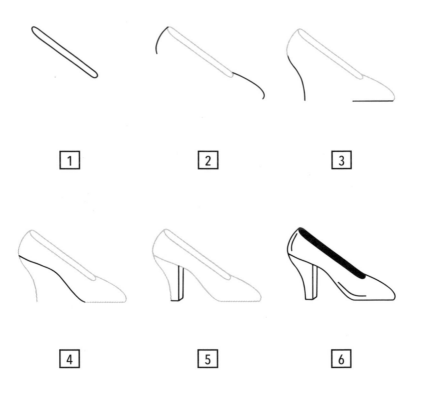

SWORD

According to the famous legend, King Arthur became king by pulling a magical sword out of a stone.

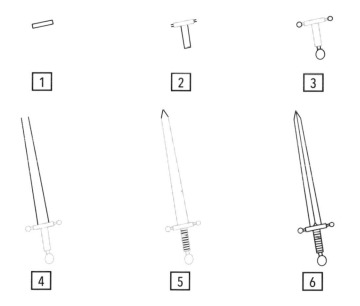

CROWN

Kings and queens wear different crowns. A king's crown usually has a pointed top, while a queen's crown is bowed in the middle.

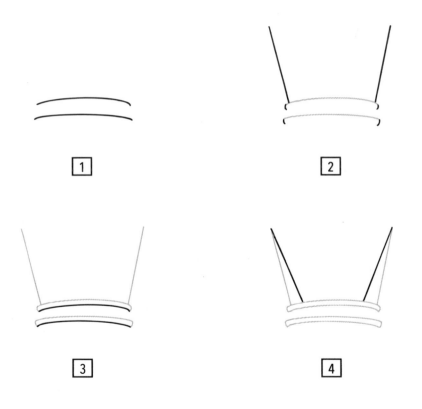

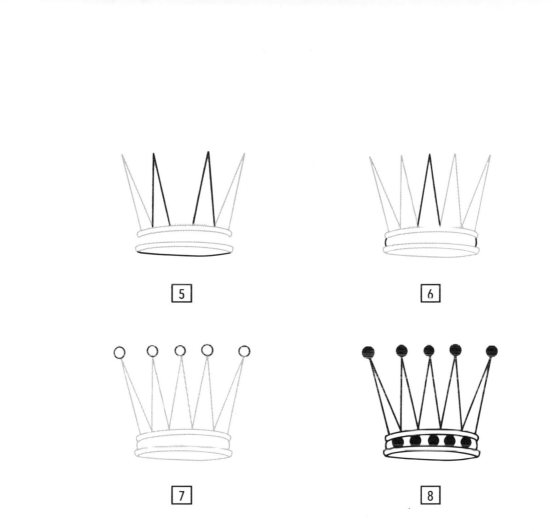

5

6

7

8

GIANT

Giants can grow to be 24 feet tall—taller than a full-grown giraffe!

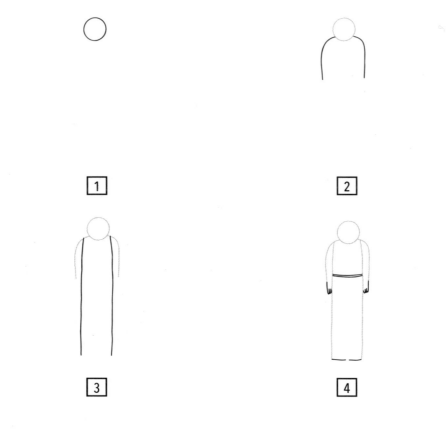

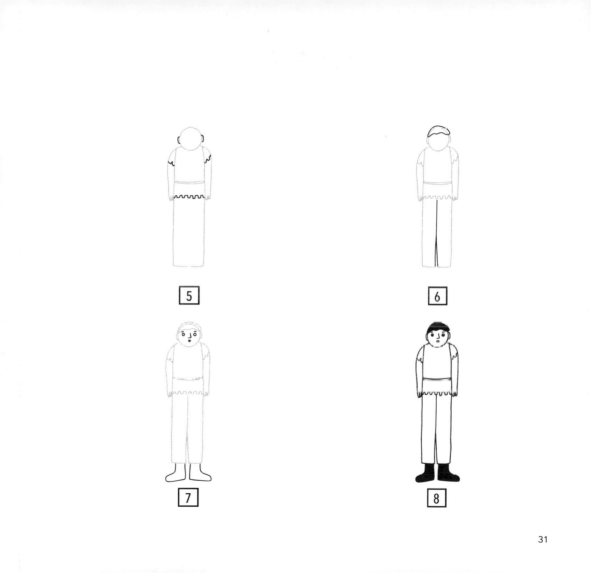

5

6

7

8

FAIRY

Fairies use their wings to fly, but they also use them to wave "hello" to each other.

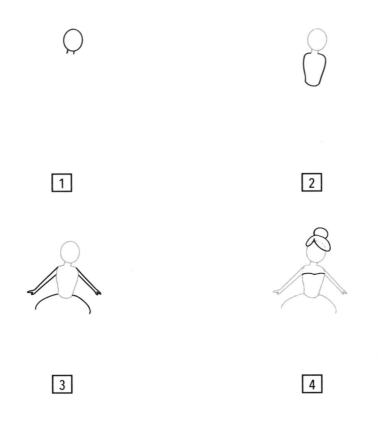

5

6

7

8

POT OF GOLD

According to Irish folklore, fairies place the pot of gold at the end of a rainbow, and the leprechauns protect it.

WITCH BROOM

In Swaziland, witches are not allowed to fly more than 150 meters above the ground.

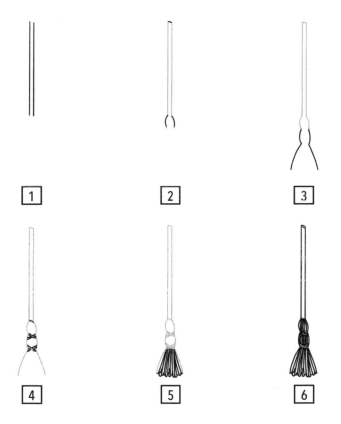

WITCH

When a group of witches gather, it's called a coven.

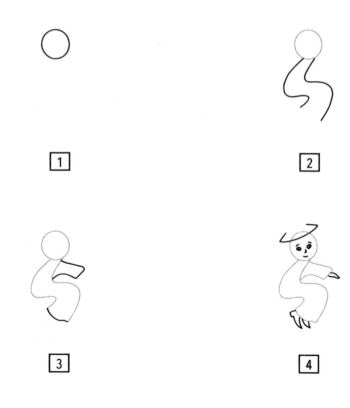

1

2

3

4

WIZARD

The modern name "wizard" comes from the Middle English word "wysard," which means "wise man."

1

2

3

4

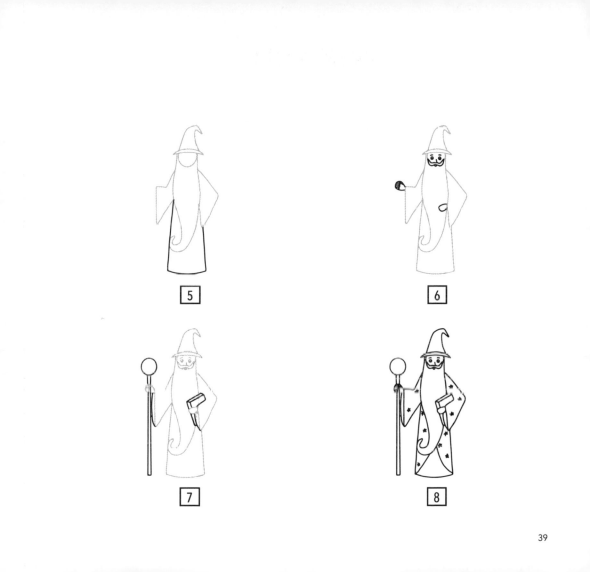

5

6

7

8

WAND

The first known references to magical wands were found in Greek mythology, in which the god Hermes used a wand to put people to sleep.

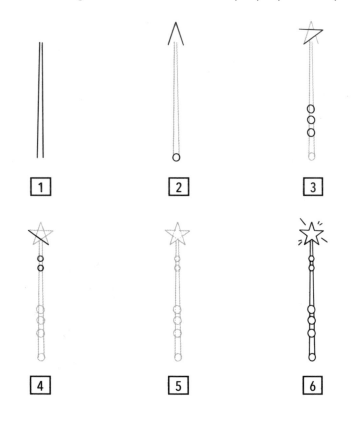

GENIE

Genies can do more than just grant wishes.
They can also fly, shapeshift, and even make themselves invisible.

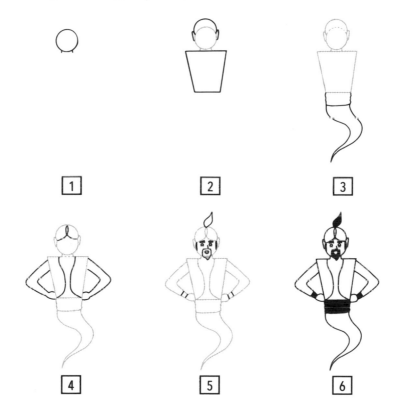

GNOME

Gnomes can live to be 400 years old, and they are believed to live all over the world.

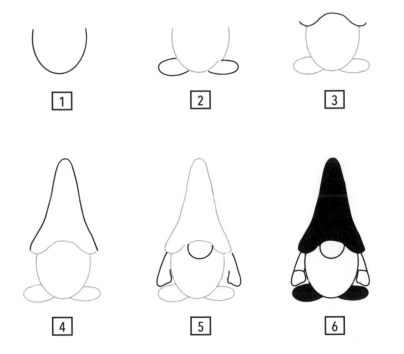

1

2

3

4

5

6

FAIRY GARDEN HOUSE

According to mythology, fairies use their front doors to travel between the human world and the fairy world.

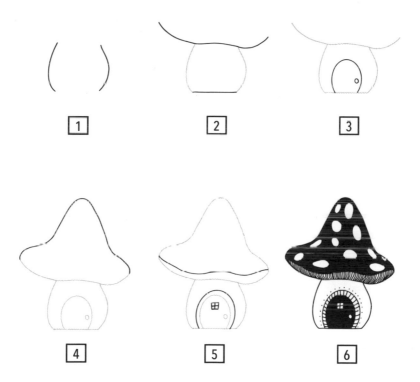

IMAGINATION

SHOOTING STAR

Shooting stars are not really stars—
they are actually meteors that can travel up to 120,000 miles per hour.

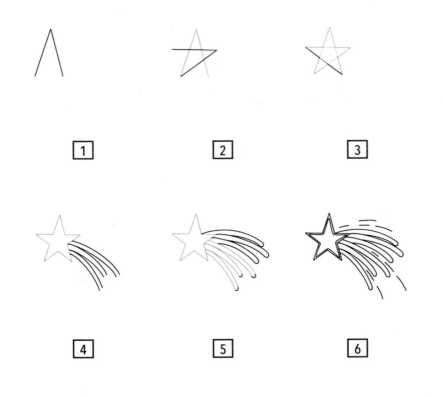

FACE ON THE MOON

Can you see a face on the moon? When people see a face on the moon, it is actually a collection of large plains of hardened lava!

BUTTERFLY

The process of a caterpillar turning into a butterfly may seem magical, but it's really just science! Caterpillars molt their skin inside cocoons until they're ready to emerge as butterflies.

RAINBOW

Because rainbows are optical illusions, no two people see the exact same rainbow.

CREATURES

PHOENIX

According to legend, a phoenix could live for 97,200 years.

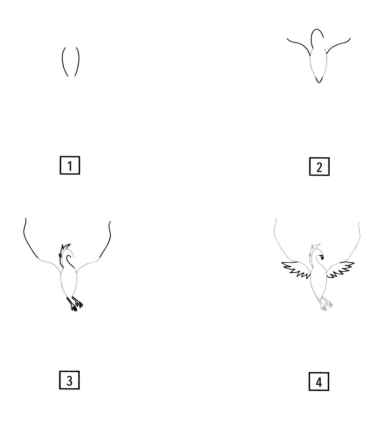

5

6

7

8

PEGASUS

In Greek mythology, there was just one Pegasus, and he was an immortal horse who could fly.

MONSTER

The word "monster" comes from the Latin word "monstrare," which means "evil omen."

1

2

3

4

5

6

OGRE

A female ogre is called an "ogress."

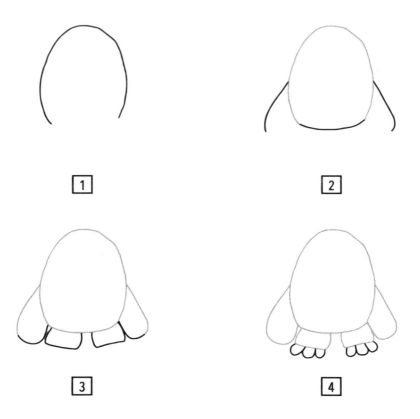

5

6

7

8

DRAGON

Real dragons do exist—but thankfully, they don't breathe fire!
Komodo dragons live on islands in Indonesia.

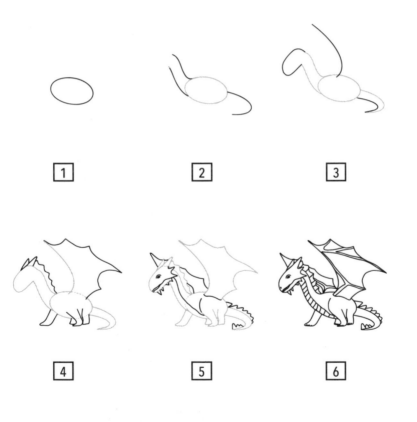

DRAGON EGG

Just like the creatures that are hatched from them, dragon eggs
can be many different colors and have fun patterns.

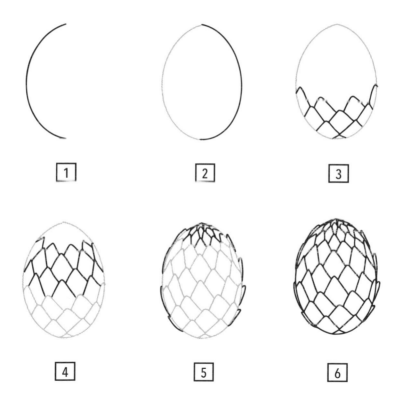

UNICORN

The name "unicorn" means "one horn,"
and these magical creatures are the official animal of Scotland.

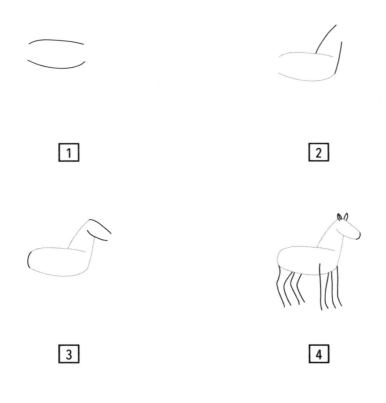

1

2

3

4

5

6

7

8

THREE-HEADED DRAGON

According to Greek mythology, Chimera was a three-headed
monster that could breathe fire and had the udders of a goat and a serpent's tail.

1

2

3

4

5

6

7

8

CYCLOPS

Cyclops only have one eye, and some legends say that this eye gives them the ability to see into the future.

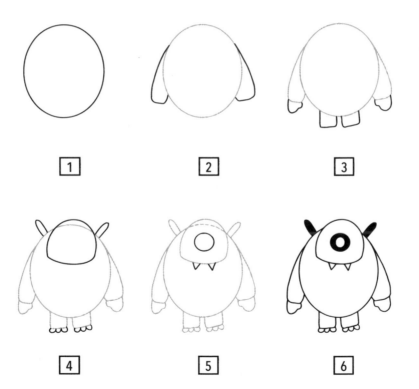

JACKALOPE

With the ability to mimic human noises, some cowboys have reported hearing these mythical rabbits sing popular campfire songs.

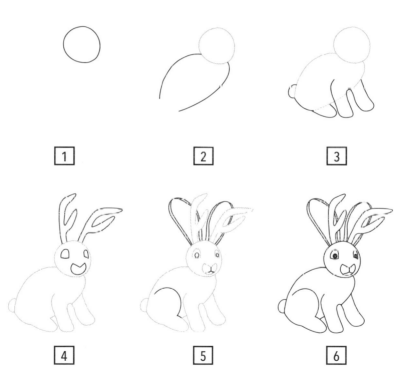

ALIEN

Because an alien sighting has never been confirmed, aliens could come in all different colors and have fun patterns on their skin. Let your imagination run wild!

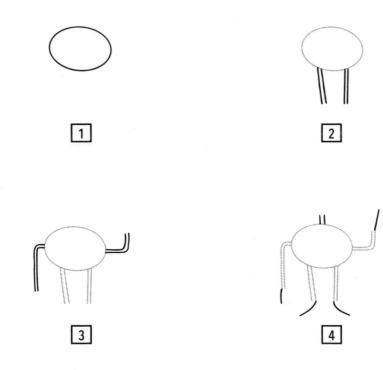

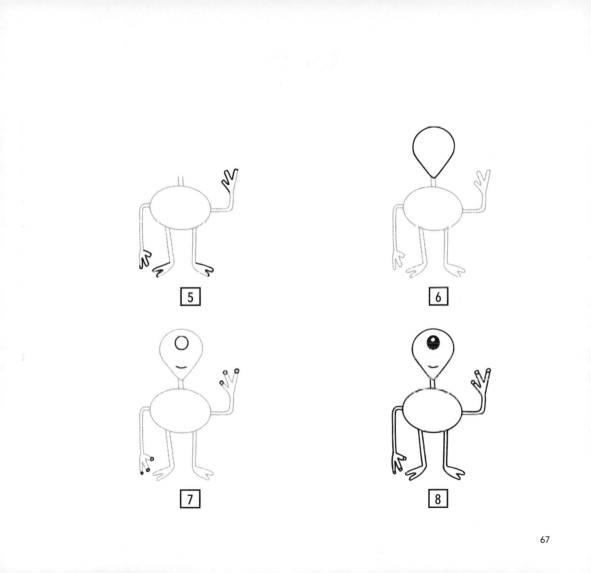

5

6

7

8

SNOW MONSTER

In Siberia, the reward for capturing a snow monster is more than $30,000 U.S. dollars.

TROLL

Trolls are the primary enemies of gnomes.
They like to make gnomes' lives as difficult as possible!

NORTH POLE

SANTA

In order to deliver presents to every child on Earth, Santa's sleigh has to travel at a speed of 1,800 miles per second.

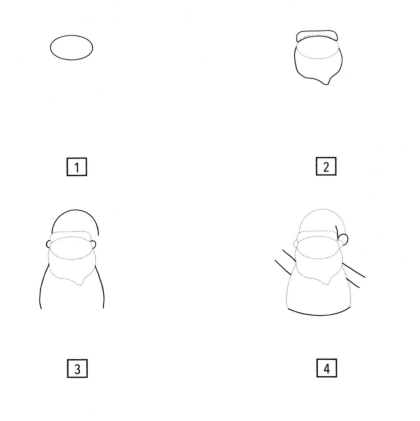

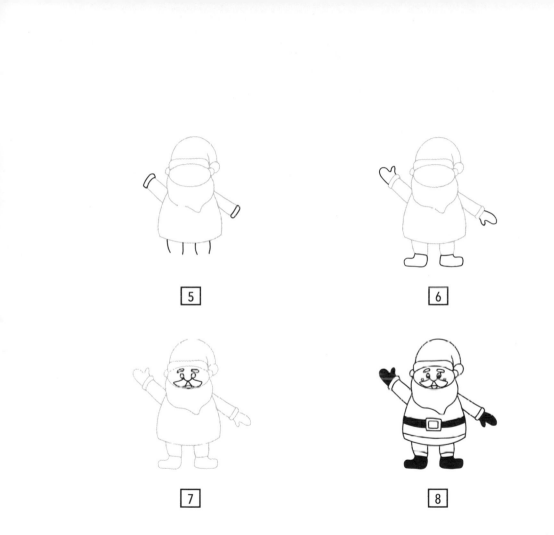

5

6

7

8

73

ELF

When they're not helping make toys, elves decorate their cottages with ornaments, lights, and gingerbread throughout the year.

1

2

3

4

5

6

7

8

REINDEER

In addition to living in the North Pole, reindeer can be found roaming around Alaska, Canada, Russia, and Scandinavia.

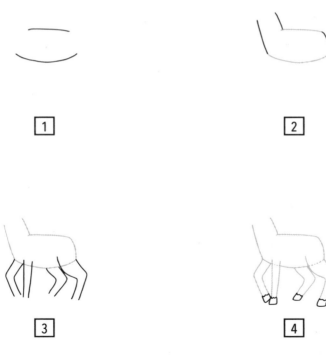

5

6

7

8

GINGERBREAD HOUSE

Did you know? The largest real-life gingerbread house
was 60 feet long and 21 feet tall!

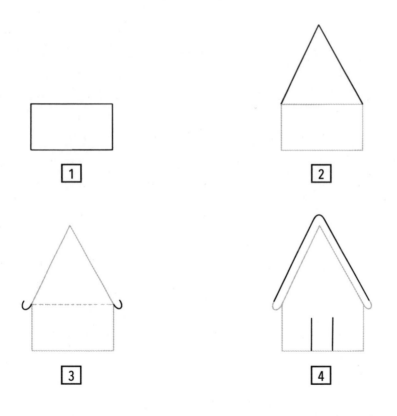

5

6

7

8

About Alli K

NAME: Alli Koch

HOME: Dallas, Texas

BIRTHDAY: March 20, 1991

FAVORITE COLOR: Black

FAVORITE FOOD: Waffle fries and a large sweet tea

JOB: I am a full-time artist! I sell my art online, paint on the side of buildings, and teach others how to draw or be creative

FAVORITE THING: A warm blanket

PETS: I have one cat named Emmie

CAR: Tahoe

FAMILY: Married to my high school sweetheart

FAVORITE ANIMAL: Cats and dolphins

FAVORITE THING TO DO: Playing board games!